PATTERN ANIMALS
PUZZLES FOR PATTERN BLOCKS

by

Sandra Mogensen and Judi Magarian-Gold

Illustrations by Michael Liberatore

INTRODUCTION

WHY USE PATTERN BLOCKS?

Pattern Blocks provide students with a concrete tool to learn how to make generalizations, see relationships and understand strategies of problem solving and logic.

As students manipulate the blocks, they work together to solve problems, check the relationships of their answers and compare ideas. Verbalizing adds an important dimension to learning. The language used to describe the designs enriches understanding and expands thinking as students explore and interact with the material and each other.

WHAT IS PATTERN ANIMALS?

PATTERN ANIMALS is a new, unique book to use with students in Grades 1-3.

The first section comprises 20 worksheets to be used with animal pages. As each of the worksheets can be used with each animal, there are hundreds of ways to explore, create and problem solve with PATTERN ANIMALS. Math activities include counting and covering tasks, sorting, graphing, sequencing, estimation and symmetry. In addition to mathematics activities, several worksheets integrate other curriculum areas: reading, oral and written language, creative writing, study skills and art.

The second section consists of 26 animal pattern puzzles. From Arnold Alligator to Zachary Zebra, children cover each animal outline with Pattern Blocks.

WHY USE PATTERN ANIMALS?

Children relate to the domestic and non-domestic animal outlines. By using the different colored blocks, children see their favorite animals change by colors, or by the number of blocks used to cover each outline. Especially motivating is the variety of ways to cover the animal outlines. Patterns are recorded and compared for each animal to help children discover the significance of area conservation.

HOW DO YOU USE PATTERN ANIMALS?

After free exploration with Pattern Blocks (building, stacking, etc.), introduce children to the animal outlines and worksheets. There are several ways this can be done:

- With younger children, use the animal outlines as puzzles - independently of the worksheets.
- Teachers can select worksheets according to age and interest. They need not be used in any particular sequence. Also, as an incentive, allow children to choose their favorite animals and complete appropriate worksheets.
- Using a variety of animal outlines and worksheets, a PATTERN ANIMALS learning center can be set up in the classroom. This gives students the freedom to choose activities and then work individually, in pairs, or small groups.

Finally, it is important to note that PATTERN ANIMALS activities provide hands-on experience, social interaction and active exploration by children. Most often, more than one answer is possible with the outlines and worksheets. This allows children to discover their own solutions and be actively involved with problem solving, while the teacher guides them through this process.

We hope you enjoy using this book as much as we enjoyed developing the animal puzzles and activities with our students, and welcome any comments or suggestions.

BLOCK SORT

Name_____

1. Choose an animal and cover it with Pattern Blocks.

2. Pick up the blocks you used to cover your animal.

3. Put the blocks in piles by shapes.

EXAMPLE

4. Write how many of each you used.

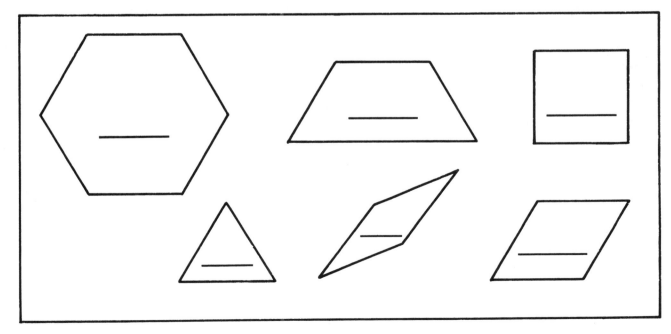

COVER UP

Name_____

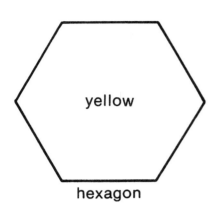
yellow
hexagon

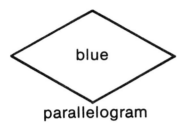
blue
parallelogram

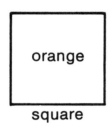
orange
square

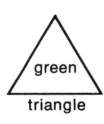
green
triangle

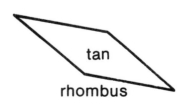
tan
rhombus

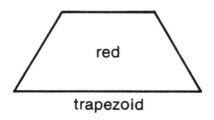
red
trapezoid

Animal Name_____

1. Cover the animal with Pattern Blocks.

2. How many blocks did you use? _____

3. Which block did you use

most?_____
least?_____
not at all?_____

4. How many different colors did you use?

_____

4

MOST BLOCKS, LEAST BLOCKS

Name_____

1. Choose three (3) animals.

2. Cover each animal using the most blocks you can. How many did you use?

3. Record your answers on the chart.

4. Cover each animal again using the least number of blocks. How many did you use?

5. Record your answers on the chart.

	Animal	Most Blocks	Least Blocks
(1)			
(2)			
(3)			

SORT THE ANIMALS

Sort the animals in the book and tally your results in the boxes below.

1. Name the animals that you would or would not like as pets.

Animals that I want as pets	Animals that I would not want as pets
_____	_____
_____	_____
_____	_____
_____	_____
_____	_____
_____	_____
_____	_____
_____	_____
_____	_____
_____	_____
_____	_____
_____	_____
_____	_____
_____	_____

2. Now choose an animal that would make a good pet or one that would not make a good pet and cover it with Pattern Blocks.

3. On another sheet of paper write about the animal you chose. Share why you chose it.

SORT THE ANIMALS (B)

Name_____

> Sort the animals in the book and tally your results in the boxes below.

1. Sort the animals by their male or female names.

Animals with male names	Animals with female names
_____	_____
_____	_____
_____	_____
_____	_____
_____	_____
_____	_____
_____	_____
_____	_____
_____	_____
_____	_____
_____	_____
_____	_____
_____	_____

2. Choose an animal with a male or female name and cover it with Pattern Blocks.

3. On another sheet of paper, write a story about how this animal got its name.

TURN AROUND

1. Work with a partner. Each of you choose two (2) animals.

2. Cover the animals with Pattern Blocks.

3. Turn your papers around carefully so the animals are upside down.

4. Decide together which animals make sense (look reasonable) when turned upside down, and which do not.

5. Write the names of the animals below.

These animals make sense upside down	These animals do not make sense upside down
_____	_____
_____	_____
_____	_____
_____	_____
_____	_____
_____	_____

COVER UP

1. Choose three (3) animals.

2. Try to cover each of the animals using only two colors. Is it possible?

3. Fill in the chart below with your answers.

	Animal	Possible (✔)	Not Possible(✔)	Which Colors?
(1)				
(2)				
(3)				

4. Can you cover one of these animals using just three colors?

    YES _____   NO _____

    Which Animal?_____

    Which Colors? _____ _____ _____

COMBINATION COVER UP

1. Choose an animal.

2. Write its name here. _____

3. Cover the animal with Pattern Blocks.

4. What different combinations of blocks did you use? Write your answers after #1 below.

5. Using other blocks how many different ways can you cover the animal? Record your answers below.

	Total Blocks	⬡	⬢	☐	△	▱	◇
(1)							
(2)							
(3)							
(4)							
(5)							

GO AROUND

1. Choose an animal and cover it with Pattern Blocks.

2. After you cover it, use more blocks to go around the edge of the paper, like a picture frame.

3. You now have a picture of your animal in a frame.

   a. Count the blocks you used for your frame. Record them below.

   b. After you have recorded the blocks in the frame, tell about your special animal to a friend.

	Animal Name _____					
Shape	⬡	△	☐	◇	⬟	◇
Number of blocks						

WHAT'S NEXT?

Name_____

This is a pattern:

And this is a pattern:

1. Choose an animal and cover it with Pattern Blocks.

2. Put the blocks you used in piles, like this:

3. Use some or all of the blocks, and make your own patterns.

4. Draw the patterns in the spaces below and explain them.

Animal _____

GUESS AND COVER

Name_____

1. Choose three (3) animals.

2. Look at the outlined animals and guess how many blocks it would take to fill each.

3. Record the names and your guesses in the chart below.

4. Cover the animals with Pattern Blocks and record the actual number it takes to fill each.

5. Find the difference between your guesses and the actual numbers.

	Animal	My Guess	Actual Number	Difference
(1)				
(2)				
(3)				

ADD THEM UP (A)

Name_____

1. Choose an animal and cover it with Pattern Blocks.

2. Some of the blocks represent a value. Using the chart below, add up the value of the blocks you used and record your answer.

Each of the following blocks has the value shown.

⬡ =6   ⬭ =3

◇ =2   △ =1

The  ◇ and the ☐ blocks have no assigned values.

3. Compare your answer with others in your class and decide who has the largest number for their animal.

Animal
name:_____

Total amount ☐

Use this space to add your numbers

ADD THEM UP (B)

1. Do this activity with two (2) other friends.

2. Each of you choose the same animal to cover with Pattern Blocks.

   Don't look at each other's animals while covering!

3. Some of the blocks represent a value. Using the chart below, add up the value of the block you used and record your answer.

   > Each of the following blocks has the value shown.
   >
   > ⬡ =6   ⬟ =3 
   >
   > ◇ =2   △ =1 
   >
   > The ◇ and the ☐ blocks have no assigned values.

   Animal _____

   Total Amount [   ]

   Use this space to add up your numbers.

4. Compare your answers with your friend's answers.

   • What are their answers? _____

   • Are they the same? YES _____ NO _____

   • Did you use different blocks? YES _____ NO _____

   • If you all have the same number, discuss why!

ANIMAL'S WORTH

Name_____

What is the worth of your animal? Make believe that some of the blocks represent a unit of money.

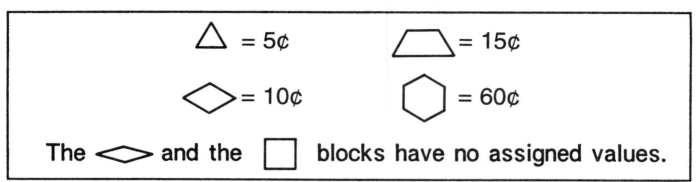

The ◇ and the ☐ blocks have no assigned values.

1. Choose an animal and cover it with Pattern Blocks.

2. Using the chart above, add up the animal's worth and record it below.

3. Try this again with 2 more animals.

4. Make believe you are selling one of the animals and write an advertisement for the <u>Pattern</u> <u>Block</u> <u>News</u>.

Animal Name	
Worth?	☐
Animal Name	
Worth?	☐
Animal Name	
Worth?	☐

PATTERN BLOCK NEWS

For Sale! _____

_____

_____

_____

_____

_____

_____

_____

UNCOVER – A GAME FOR TWO PLAYERS

1. Choose an animal.

2. Cover it with blocks.

3. Take turns removing blocks from the animal.

4. When it is your turn, you may remove 1 or 2 blocks.

5. Continue taking turns.

6. The winner is the player who removes the last block.

7. Keep score below.

8. Play the game again using other animals.

	Players	No. of Wins (Tally)
1)		
2)		

Which animals did you use for UNCOVER?

_____ _____ _____

_____ _____ _____

MIRROR REFLECTION Name_____

1. Choose an animal pattern, but do not cover it with Pattern Blocks.

2. Put a mirror down the middle of the animal, like this:

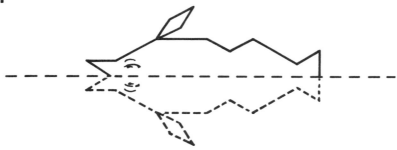

3. Does your animal look whole when you look through the mirror?

4. How many other animals look whole when you look at them through the mirror?

5. Put a check ✓ by a letter if the animal looks whole when you look through the mirror.

A __	K __	U __
B __	L __	V __
C __	M __	W __
D __	N __	X __
E __	O __	Y __
F __	P __	Z __
G __	Q __	
H __	R __	
I __	S __	
J __	T __	

...AND MIRROR MAKES TWO

Name_____

1. Choose an animal and cover it with Pattern Blocks.

2. Place a mirror on one side of your animal.

EXAMPLE:

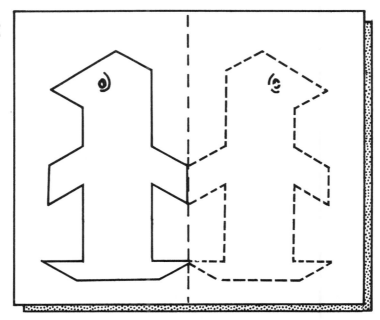

3. Look at the animal's reflection in the mirror.

4. Use the same kinds and number of blocks and build the shape you see in the mirror.

5. Check your mirror as you build to see if you are correct.

6. Choose one (1) more animal and build its reflection. Check with the mirror.

7. Which animals did you choose for this activity?

_____   _____

_____   _____

REMAKE

1. Choose one (1) animal and cover it with Pattern Blocks.

2. Show the animal to a partner.

3. Take your pieces off the animal and give them to your partner.

4. Say to your partner:

"I MADE IT...
NOW YOU MAKE IT
WITH MY PIECES."

5. Take turns doing this task. If time permits, try another one.

ANIMAL FACTS

Choose an animal you would like to know more about. You will need an encyclopedia or a book about animals.

Cover the animal with Pattern Blocks.

Now, answer the questions.

Name of the animal _____

How many blocks did you use? _____

How many different colors did you use?_____

_____

What does your animal like to eat? _____

Where does it live? _____

_____

Who are its enemies? _____

_____

Would this animal make a good pet? _____

Why or why not?_____

_____

DESIGN AN ANIMAL

Name_____

1. Choose an animal and cover it with Pattern Blocks.

2. Which animal did you choose? _____

3. How many blocks did you use? _____

4. Use these same blocks to make another animal that begins with the <u>same</u> <u>letter</u>.

EXAMPLE:

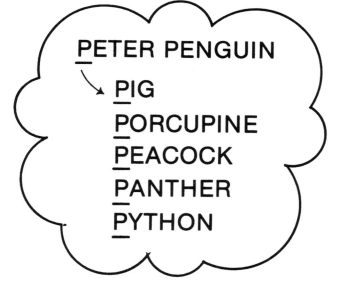

<u>P</u>ETER <u>P</u>ENGUIN

  ↘ <u>P</u>IG

<u>P</u>ORCUPINE

<u>P</u>EACOCK

<u>P</u>ANTHER

<u>P</u>YTHON

5. On another sheet of paper, draw and color your animal.

6. Give your new animal a name and write it on your paper.

Arnold Alligator

Bernie Bear

Carla Crab

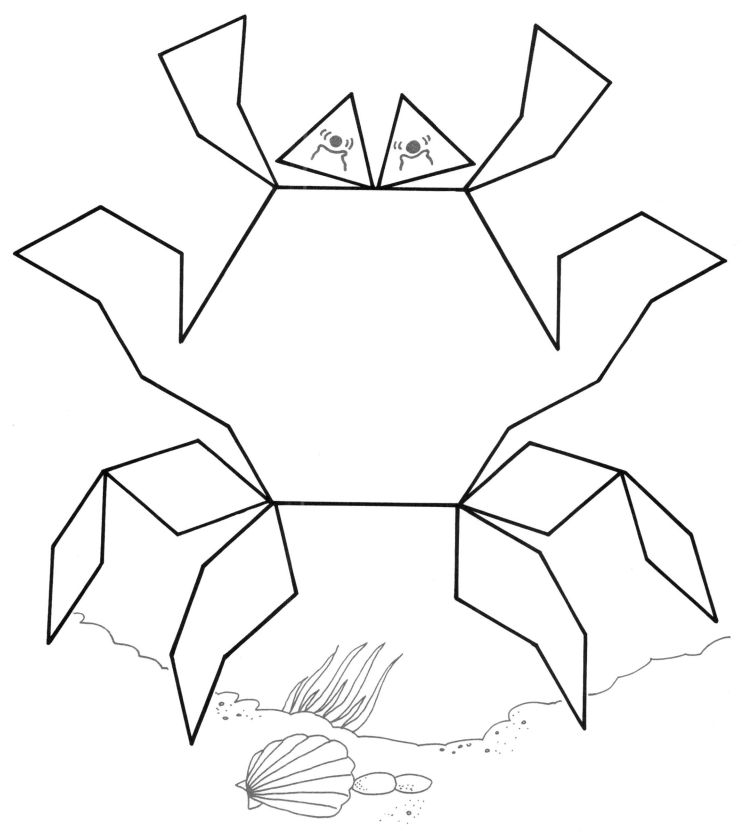

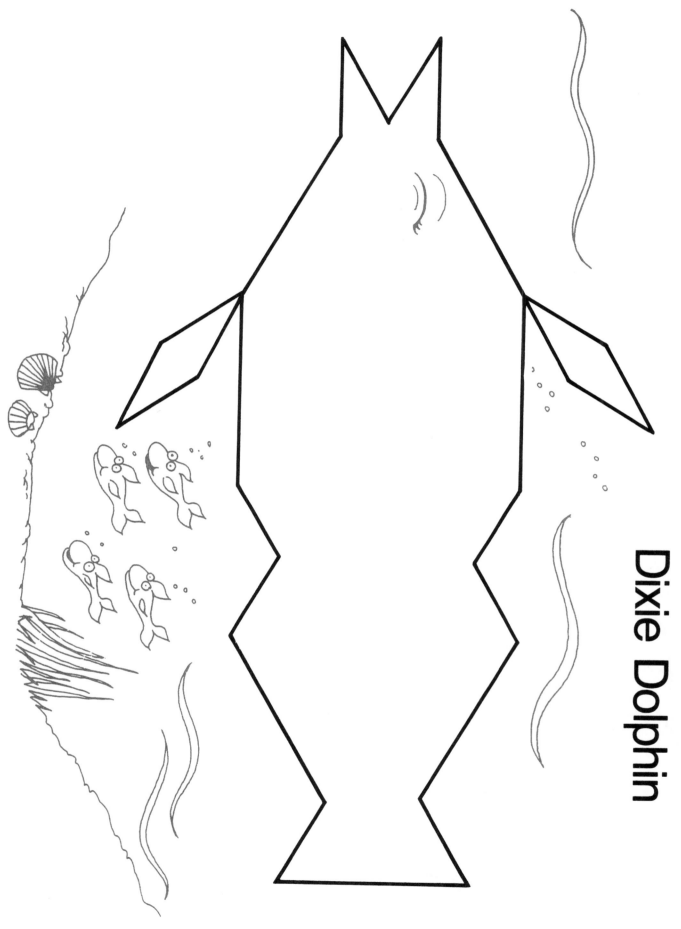

Dixie Dolphin

Ernie Elephant

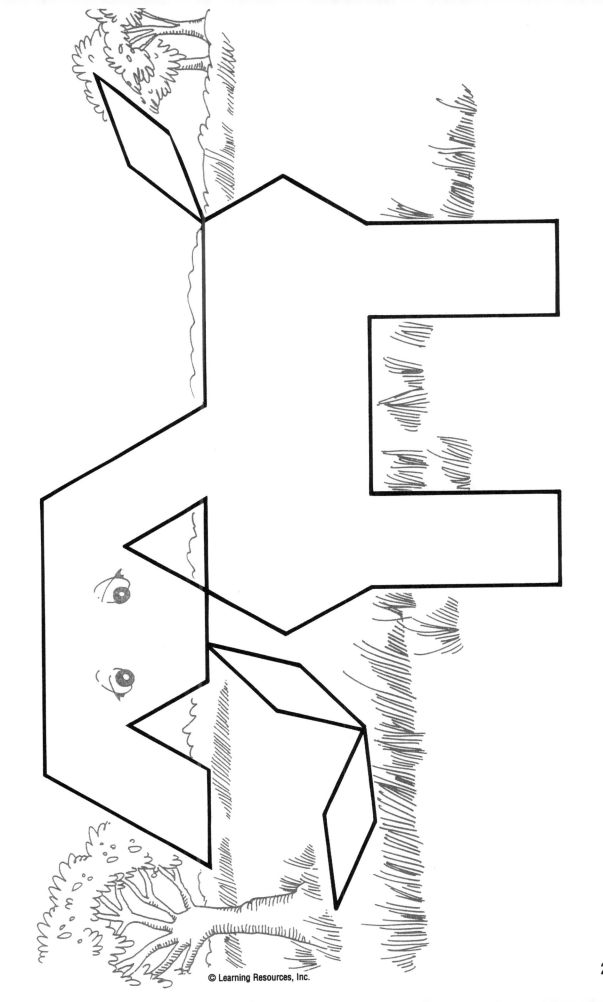

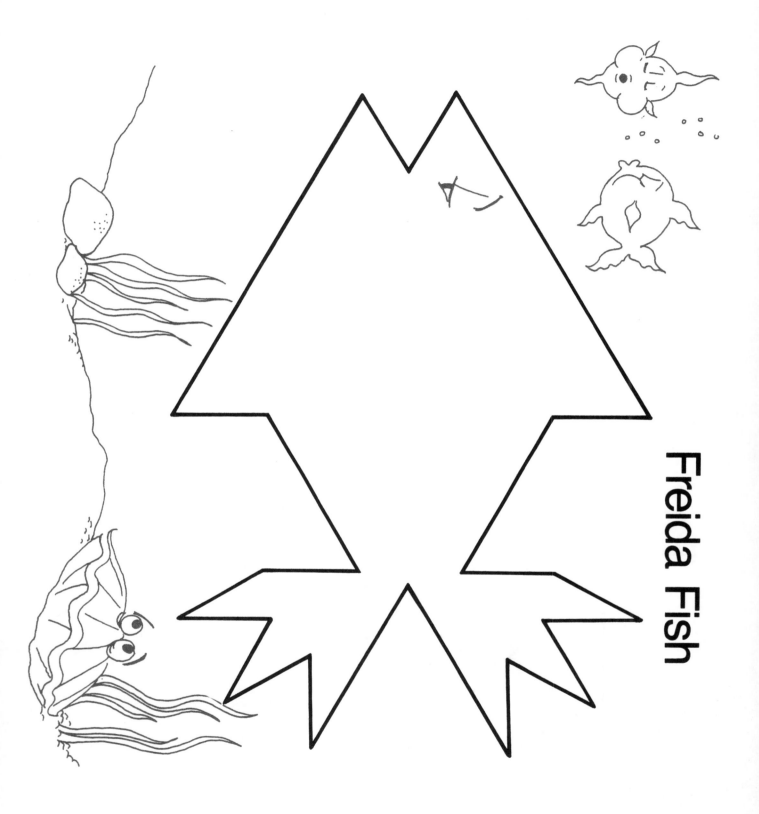

Freida Fish

Ginger Giraffe

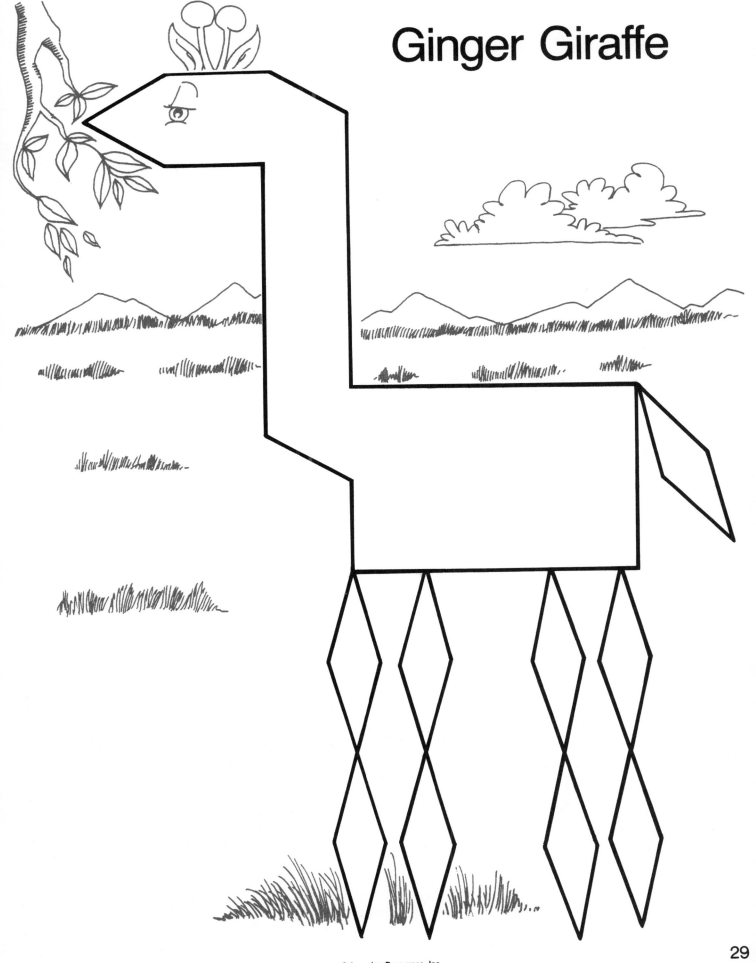

29

Harry Horse

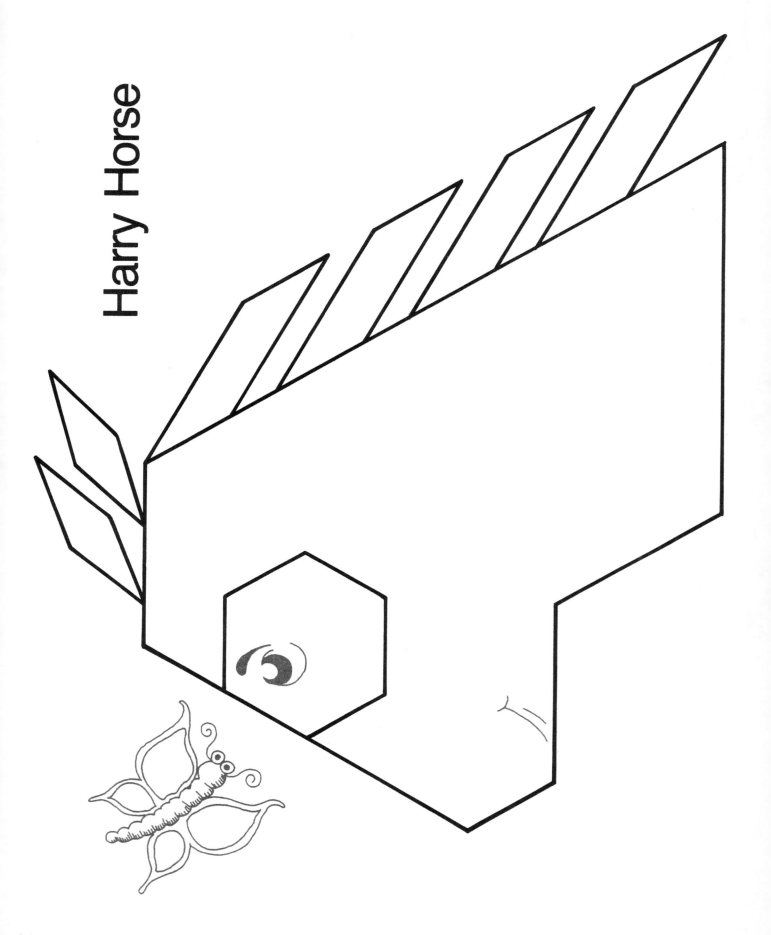

Izzy Impala

31

Josephine Jaguar

Kelly Kangaroo

Leon Lion

34

Maggie Monkey

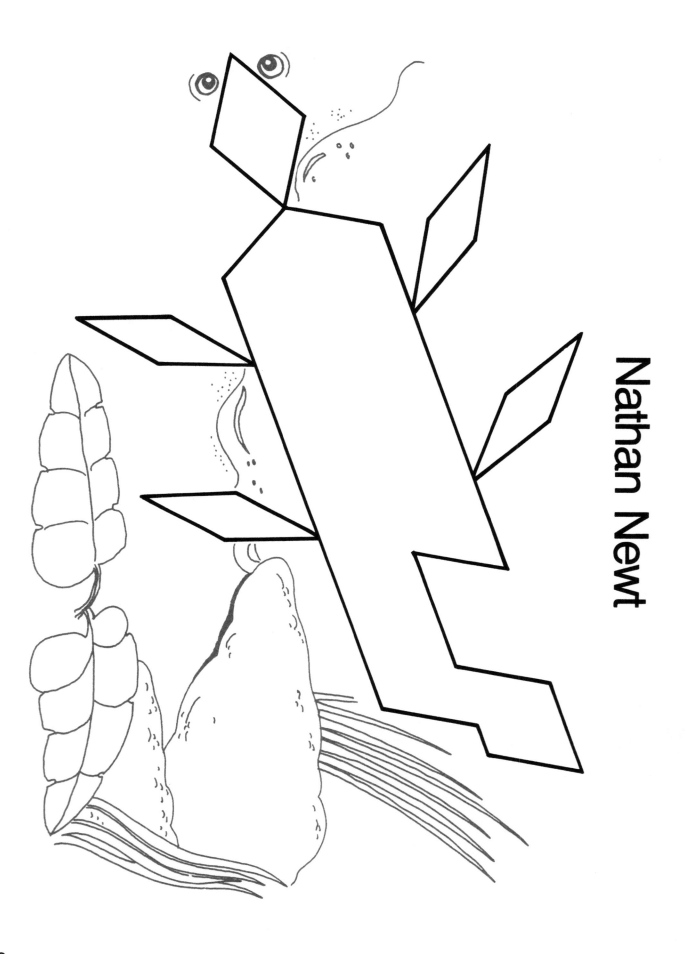

Nathan Newt

Oscar Owl

37

Peter Penguin

Quincy Quetzal

Rhonda Rabbit

Spencer Spider

41

Tanya Turtle

Ulysses Unau

Victor Vulture

Wanda Walrus

45

Xavier Xenopus

Yolanda Yak

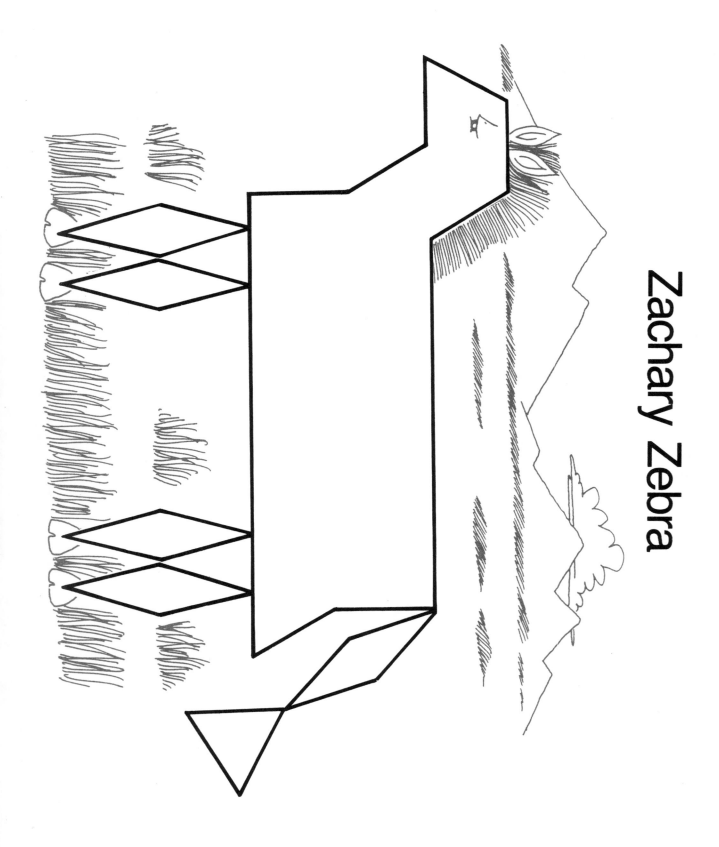

Zachary Zebra